I0410736

Feminist Coloring Book For Adults

Feminist inspired coloring book for women. A celebration of the beauty of the female body with a comic twist.

by The Coloring Book People

ISBN-13: 978-1537647753

ISBN-10: 153764775X

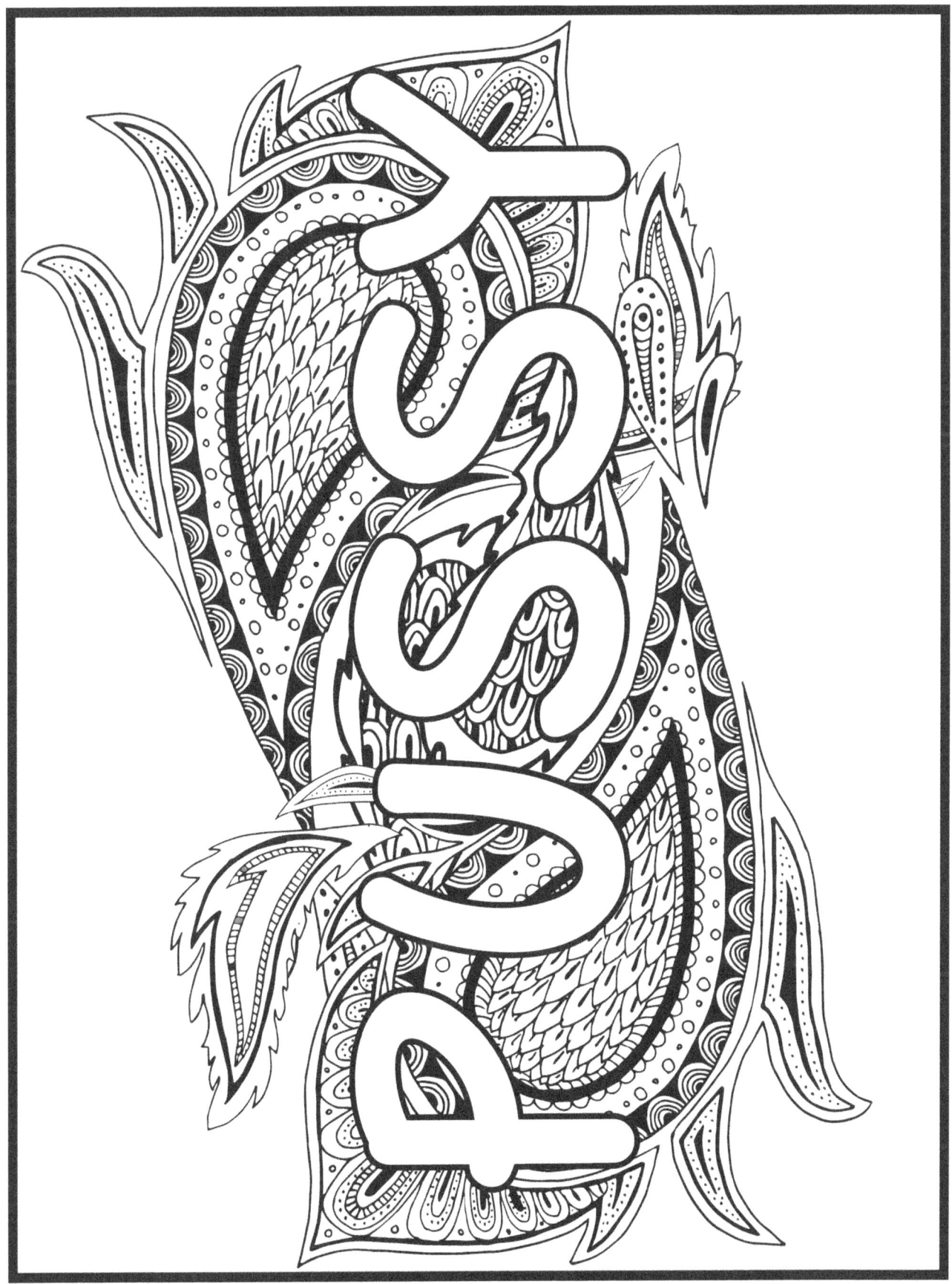

COLOR TEST PAGE

COLOR TEST PAGE

www.ingramcontent.com/pod-product-compliance
Lightning Source LLC
Chambersburg PA
CBHW081758280526
45789CB00008B/2900